D0255533

The In-Sourcing Handbook

Where and How to Find the Happiness You Deserve

**Arlene Englander, LCSW
and Howard Englander**

ISBN: 1478192631
ISBN-13: 9781478192633

Library of Congress Control Number: 2012912257
CreateSpace, North Charleston, SC

Happiness is like a butterfly which, when pursued,
is always beyond our grasp,
but, if you will sit down quietly, may alight upon you.

Nathaniel Hawthorne

For my clients, whose courage and unflagging resolve continue to inspire me.

CONTENTS

What Exactly Is "In-Sourcing"?   1

Intention   3

Opening Our Eyes To A Life Of Joy And Fulfillment   5

Making The Unknown, Known   7

Body, Mind, Spirit / Thoughts, Feelings, Behaviors   11

How And Why To Surf?   13

A Note About God   15

The Significance Of '40' Days   17

Commitment   19

Begin!   21

Body   23

Wake up — Literally!   25

Water, Water . . .   27

Exercise, the Natural Anti-Depressant   29

Think About What You Eat   31

Control Your Breath - Control Your Emotions   35

Time Out for Play Time   37

Pamper Yourself   39

The Extraordinary Power of Laughter   41

Mind   45

Live In the Now   47

Gratitude as Attitude   51

Be Inspired   53

Improve Your Eyesight   55
Accept and Detach   57
(Non) Judgment Day   59
The "Good" Good-bye   61
Forgive... and Flourish   63
Paint. Draw. Dream.   67
Mean What You Say   69
Less Facebook - More Face to Face   71
Test the Assumptions   73
Clean Your Closet, and Speak Your Truth   75
Healthy Boundaries   77
Childhood Dues   79
Be Flexible   81
Help Someone Help Himself   83
Receiving is a Vital Part of Giving   85
Whistle a Happy Tune   87
Know When to Fold 'Em   89
Spirit   91
Blessings   93
Ponder the Paradox   95
More Than Just Energy—Vitality!   99
Marvel at the Miracles   101
What's in a Name? Everything!   105
The Gold to be Found in Silence   109
Be of Service   113
A Five Minute, Daily 'Sabbath'   115
The Merging Of Body, Mind And Spirit   117
Final Words   123
Visualizations   125
Balancing the Chakras   127
Replace A Negative Thought With A Positive One 129
The Authors' Journeys   133

WHAT EXACTLY IS "IN-SOURCING"?

Most of us who work or have worked in the corporate world are familiar with the concept of "out-sourcing." When a job situation puts a strain on the resources readily at hand, we bring in outside experts to help. Just phone calls away are technical consultants who can develop systems for computer networks, engineering firms to conduct feasibility studies or independent arbitrators to review contract disputes. You simply go on-line to find the expert's number and pick up the phone to make the call.

Wouldn't it be wonderful if we could deal with sadness and dejection the same way? For every personal problem that caused us to become unhappy, we'd have a number to call to bring in an expert to help us solve the problem and return to a happy state.

The fact is, this system is already in place twenty-four hours a day, seven days a week! It makes use of the business world's out-sourcing techniques, but the difference is, you go inside - instead of outside - for the help you need. It's

1

called "in-sourcing" - or turning to the resources that reside within you when a personal situation arises that disrupts your inner happiness and diminishes the joy and fulfillment you deserve.

The resources we refer to exist as components of our body, our mind and our spirit. If you know how to look for them, you will find them there. The pages that follow will guide you.

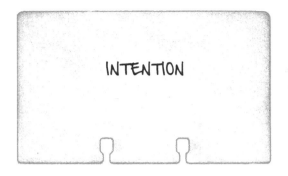

INTENTION

Why write this book?

Over and over again, to new clients and long-time clients, to friends and family, to anyone who seeks my guidance on how to live life more fully, I find myself explaining the one basic principle inherent to achieving personal happiness: *within us, available right now, we have everything we need to achieve a life of joy and fulfillment.*

We don't have to "search" outside of ourselves for the components of a happy and meaningful life. The path leads inward. What we have to do is allow the deep, joyful light within us to emerge from behind the false beliefs and negative programming of our past.

Every spiritual tradition has its own way of expressing this truism. Buddhists call it our True Nature; Christians call it Christ Consciousness; Sufis call it One with the Beloved; Kabbalists call it the Holy Spark of Light; and yogis call it the Self or the yoking of the finite with the infinite.

But as Groucho Marx said, "If you don't accept the premise, you cannot get the joke." You have to believe that the source of wellness is within you. The In-sourcing Handbook provides practical, everyday ways to open an accessible doorway to that deep, joyful light within all of us. It's meant to be used as an instruction manual offering practical exercises to help guide you through the outer layer - the ego self - into the inner realm - the spiritual self - so you can experience, even for a fleeting moment, who you really are at your core.

How you choose to live your life is up to you. Each and every day you make decisions that bring you happiness or sadness. The intention of The In-sourcing Handbook is to offer simple, hands-on ways to choose more wisely. You do not have to change who you are. All you have to do is clear away the veils that keep you from who you are *already*. Use this book as the first step in that process.

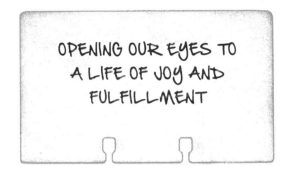

OPENING OUR EYES TO
A LIFE OF JOY AND
FULFILLMENT

What is the 'alarm' that wakes us up; motivates us to be in the present, wide open to a life with all its joys fully avail able? It can come in a variety of ways: illness, disappointment, depression... or simply opening our eyes - becoming aware of and confronting the question: "Is this all there is to life?"

Sooner or later, most of us recognize, "I am leading my life by rote, following someone else's rules. I feel as if I am playing a role rather than listening to my inner self." Haven't you experienced the feeling that you go through the day split between how others want you to be, and how you really feel?

Most people have layers of physical, emotional and spiritual blocks that prevent them from connecting with their true, basic nature. When these barriers are removed, integration can take place between the outer and inner Self, and life can be lived to the fullest. Instead of being driven by neediness, fear, loneliness, anger and shame, a change occurs and we learn to love ourselves unconditionally. And when that transformation takes place, life is lived with joy and fulfillment – we are happy!

This handbook is a first step in making the shift from simply tolerating life as a victim of circumstance, to celebrating life as an active participant responsible for choices made and actions taken.

MAKING THE UNKNOWN, KNOWN

My intention for writing this Handbook is simple - to make you aware of your hidden source of happiness, that place of inner peace existent deep within you, known as the Infinite.

You don't have to be "smart" or wear a turban or devote endless hours to "get there." The handbook's simple practices enable you to open the door to a world that makes itself known when you let go of ego-driven goals and allow the energy flow of the universe to lift you and carry you to a loftier sense of your connection to the source of creation itself.

You don't have to listen to CDs, buy a course promising enlightenment, or join a group. Everything you need to achieve personal happiness is within you. (I call my therapy practice Wellness Source, because each client is the source of his or her own wellness). Simply do one of the exercises for 40 days (the length of time that it takes to create a habit according to Yogic tradition), and you will be there.

It's fair to ask, "Where exactly is 'there'?" Just left of the gall bladder? Below the belly button? Alongside the medulla oblongata? And how do we find it?

The logical mind in the left hemisphere of the brain is our rational control booth. Think of it as "laser energy," a sharp, clear bolt of energy that gets us from A to Z in the quickest, most efficient way. The creative mind in the right hemisphere of the brain holds our memories, feelings and emotions. Think of it as "magnetic energy," a series of concentric circles that connect all sorts of seemingly unrelated parts, thereby creating new and unique combinations (the so-called 'creative process').

Science has come a long way in mapping how the brain works, but more wonders remain to be uncovered. I believe that someday soon there will be a 'chart' of how our right brain creates a sense of what we call "God" or our spiritual Self. Typically we become "spiritual" when we are moved by values that seem to reveal a meaning or power beyond our visible world, such as beauty, love, or inherent goodness. An idea or practice is spiritual when it creates a heart-felt relationship to a feeling of being connected with a larger reality removed from individual desire. There is a sense of Oneness with nature or the cosmos; or with what some call divinity. Common to the sense of spirituality is the unseen nature of its existence. We "know" it's there but you can't measure or weigh concepts such as love, compassion and forgiveness or prove a belief that everything in the universe is mutually dependent.

So how do we make the unknown, known? Where is "there"? Dear reader, you *are* there.

At the end of my Kundalini yoga (as taught by Yogi Bhajan) teaching program I took an oath: I am not a woman, I am not a man, I am not a person, I am not myself... I am a teacher.

The point being made – put aside the labels that people use to identify you. They are merely invented descriptions of who you are, derived by the ego from perceptions associated with the characterization (bookish students are nerds, cheerleaders are ditzy... you get the idea). The oath I took says, teaching is removed from gender and self-professed images of the teacher. When you teach you are simply the teacher, all artifice removed.

Of course the appellatives by which we are known remain: when I teach I continue to be a parent, a wife, a friend, a therapist... but my goal is to be authentic, to deliver the core of the lesson rather than the shadow of my ego.

You are "there" when you learn to separate the external perceptions of who you are from the authentic Self that is infinitely more encompassing and expansive. A simple Spanish lesson will help me explain what I mean. In English we say "I AM sad." as if our very being is sad. In Spanish, it is "Yo tengo triste," translated literally, "I HAVE sadness."

If you HAVE something, you can dispossess yourself of it. It is not you, so you can hold it and observe it. Observation gives you distance and allows you to disengage; it allows you to be aware of the present. Said simply, when you hold it at arm's length, you can SEE it, you are NOT it. And that gives you the power to acknowledge the feeling, but not be absorbed by it. Your authentic Self remains available. Free from the self-important pandering of the ego, you can access what the Buddhists call your true nature. You are, in effect, "there," swimming in the sea of your inner self. And that is pure happiness.

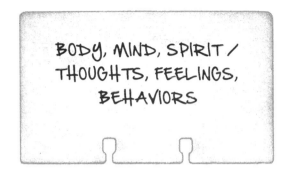

BODY, MIND, SPIRIT /
THOUGHTS, FEELINGS,
BEHAVIORS

It surprises me when people are insulted when someone tells them that a physical pain or ailment might be psychosomatic. Are not the body, mind and spirit connected?

As I explain to my clients, we **feel** in our body. It is where our emotions are amplified as sensations. We **think** in our mind. It is the storehouse of our thoughts, both conscious and subconscious. And our spirit is our **witness**, our conscious awareness. It is the part of us that observes our behavior and gives us free choice... determines who we are at the core, defining our values, morals and character.

To separate those aspects of the Self keeps us from being fully present. When all three work together in harmony, when all three are balanced, then we are able to live more fully and completely, thus more happily.

Just as the body, mind and spirit are interconnected, so are thoughts, feelings and behaviors. This relationship was beautifully illustrated in a segment of 60 Minutes a few years back about the Venezuelan Youth Orchestra. It showed how learning to play an orchestral instrument changed the lives of poor children in dramatic fashion... the music touching their spirits... which affected their way of thinking about themselves... which opened them to new ways of behaving... and coming up with options other than being condemned to their fate in the ghetto.

At this juncture, despite the analogy, invariably my clients interject, "Arlene, I understand that I can look at evidence and change my mind about something, and I can see how my behavior might change as a result. But how can you change an emotion when it is not coming from the soothing strings of the violin section, but when the stress it is causing rages inside you like a churning ocean?"

"Can you surf?" I ask. "I don't mean the Atlantic or Pacific Oceans, I mean in the ocean of your own consciousness?"

Consider an emotion as a wave of energy. If we can ride that wave, we will be in control of it rather than pulled under by its force. Imagine having waded into the "real" ocean and a big wave is coming. You have three choices: dig in and attempt to withstand the force of the wave... and the next wave, and the next (denial); duck under and attempt to avoid the wave's force... and the next wave and the next (addiction); or surf the wave and ride it safely to shore as its force dissipates and deposits you safely on the beach.

Each and every day we face situations where stress is inevitable. We can dig in and fight the roiling emotions, hide and avoid them, or surf the feelings and prevent them from gathering force.

HOW AND WHY TO SURF?

When we are adrift at sea and under stress, we trigger our *sympathetic* nervous system, which is meant to keep us in survival mode. Struggling to stay afloat, the turmoil limits our options. Our only choices are flight, fight, freeze or fragment.

When we are ashore, calm and safe, the *parasympathetic* nervous system is activated. Responses are rooted in relaxation rather than acute anxiety. We now have infinite choices of behavior, not just the limiting 4 F's.

Taking control of our breathing is the only way to trigger our parasympathetic nervous system. If we control our breath, we control how we feel. And since feelings, thoughts and behaviors are interrelated…then we can control our own destiny.

Sit quietly and notice where in your body you feel the tension. Remember that the tension is something you "have," it is not who you "are." Give the tension a color and shape to help you detach it from your body, simply observing

13

it as an image in your mind and noting on a scale of 1 to 10 the level of your feelings triggered by the picture you have created. Now just breathe and watch the image. Breathe and watch. Breathe and watch. Given your full attention the image will change color and/or shape. Just breathe and watch. The color will change its hue; the shape will get bigger or smaller. The stressful tension you have pictured will either get very strong and then dissipate… or get very weak and then dissipate. But one way or the other, it will dissipate!

Now that you are able to surf your emotions rather than be drowned or distracted by them, you find yourself safely at the shore. So what's so great about being there? Perhaps you miss the excitement of struggling in the water never knowing what to expect next.

I suppose if you want to be at the mercy of something other than your own self, the ocean of chaos sounds like the perfect place to be. However, if you want to be calm and in control of your own destiny, the shore is the preferred option.

A NOTE ABOUT GOD

Throughout this handbook you'll find many references to "God." Most assuredly, no one-size-fits-all definition of the concept is intended. That is for each individual to provide in keeping with their own upbringing, resultant faith and continuing intellectual pondering.

I merely use the word as a short hand to site the spiritual connection we seek to make to our Higher Self.

No book can encompass what "God" is, or be presumptuous enough to describe the entity... when in fact it is beyond measurement or definition. I use Yogi Bhajan's acronym: G.O.D. as the universal energy that Generates, Organizes and Delivers/Destroys... that is to say, the fundamental, cosmic principle that animates what otherwise would be clay.

THE SIGNIFICANCE OF '40' DAYS

We are what we repeatedly do.
Excellence, therefore, is not an act, but a habit.
Aristotle

The number 40 has significance in many religions and traditions. It appears frequently in many ancient and religious texts.

During Noah's flood it rained for forty days and forty nights. Lent lasts for forty days. Moses was on the mountain for forty days and nights. Jesus was seen on earth forty days after his crucifixion. Muslims mourn their dead for forty days. And as a Kundalini yoga teacher, I was taught that 40 days is the minimum requirement for establishing a new habit. (To confirm the habit, it takes 90 days; by 120 days, the habit is who you are; by 1000 days, you have mastered the new behavior. But let's take it slow - committing to 40 days is the first step.)

Why commit to anything? Completing a commitment shows you have character; that you can achieve what you have set out to do. This sense of achievement leads to a feeling of happiness, in spite of, or perhaps because of the difficulty of the process.

The important thing is do SOMETHING to wake up the energy - the life force - that is the gift with which we have been blessed. We have to remind ourselves that life itself is a miracle. We are blessed with the physical abilities to taste, hear, smell and the ability to connect spiritually with every manifestation of what it means to be alive! That connection opens the heart to unrestrained joy and lights the pathway toward fulfillment of your complete, authentic life, validating who you are and were meant to be.

COMMITMENT

Dear reader, you are not the only one who "puts off" the chores and everyday tasks that make up life's routine. How many times have I set my intention to write this book and how many times have I procrastinated! A countless number; I have notes that go as far back as the year 2000! Why did I procrastinate? Why does anyone?

Usually the reason is the existence of some form of fear we don't want to recognize, an unsettling worry that our performance won't be good enough or on the flip side, *will* be good enough, thereby creating expectation of continued competency. Think about a chore as simple as cleaning the car or making the bed. A spick and span car or the tight hospital corners of a neatly made bed says something about us – we're orderly, responsible, organized and disciplined. Those are complimentary adjectives but a degree of stress accompanies them – they represent standards that you must meet lest you be viewed as a disappointment, so you're a slob if you don't and under pressure if you do, fear of failure and fear of success being flip sides of the same coin. And so we avoid the risk of disappointment/achievement by putting the "To Do" list on the bottom of the pile and allowing inertia to stifle the feelings we are reluctant to face.

But a job worth doing is worth doing **wrong.** That is to say, we all get stuck once in a while. Fortunately there is a straightforward way to start your energy flowing and create a sense of achievement rather than limitation. The trick: baby steps, little bites, small accomplishments. Simply moving in the right direction - the very act of getting started – literally sets the mind in motion and creates momentum that grows with each step. If the garage has been a mess for months, clean one shelf of the refrigerator; if it's been years since you organized the family albums, make a call to your out of town sister; if your closet is overflowing with last season's wardrobe, take your shirts to the laundry. The simplest action starts the forward motion and begins the interaction among thoughts and feelings and behaviors, the smallest change in one leading to similar change in the others. So you see, it's not farfetched to connect your newly cleaned car to a new, more expansive sense of self-esteem!

So turn the page. The best way to get started is to get started!

BEGIN!

This handbook offers you opportunities to create a daily routine for nurturing your spiritual Self, guiding you on the path to a life of joy and fulfillment. In a world where the premium is on achieving material gain, it provides the basis for living life separate from the competition for salary and position, yet paradoxically, frees you from your restrictions and gives you confidence to succeed.

There is no one way to best use the handbook but here is my suggestion. For the next forty days commit to a daily scanning of the themes discussed in the BODY, MIND and SPIRIT chapters. Select the one that resonates with you on that day, and do it! For forty days, choose a topic each day and follow the directions. Forty days! No excuses! Forty days, without break, be it a concrete activity such as the *Cold Shower* in the morning or a contemplative pursuit such as the goal to *Forgive and Flourish*. You will be astonished how good you feel when your resolve is rewarded. A habit will have been formed! You will have succeeded in accomplishing a goal that you set and had the ability to achieve through the strength of your perseverance. The triumph will be yours and yours alone. It will speak to your strength of character; your personal integrity; the attributes that reside *within* you and provide the foundation for the inner happiness that expands exponentially with each pathway you set out on and complete.

Some days will be harder than others. Frequently you'll be tempted to quit along the way. What keeps me from faltering is the journal I keep, where I write briefly each day about my feelings. It takes only a few moments to pause and appraise the situation, and to renew my commitment.

The In-Sourcing Handbook is an introduction to Transformation. When you feel ready – you will know intuitively - turn to the section at the conclusion of the book (Merging of Body, Mind and Spirit) and begin the next phase of your journey… into time without end.

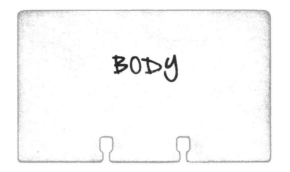

BODY

The health of the body can have a dramatic impact on one's ability to enjoy life to the fullest. It's the starting place for the in-sourcing process, the foundation that must be in place as you learn how and where to find the happiness you deserve.

The exercises are easy to perform. But don't overlook them because of their simplicity and familiarity. Inner happiness relies on a balance of body, mind and spirit, an interacting system that works in harmony. The body is the base of the pyramid, its health reflected as a robust intellect and emotional well being.

WAKE UP — LITERALLY!

Starting the day with a shower is not a new idea. But it can become something significantly more than a skin cleanser when you give the tap a sharp turn toward *cold*. A cold shower is an ancient yogic technology that has numerous physical and psychological benefits, cleaning your organs as well as being a brisk wake-up call – literally.

Every moment of every day will not be a walk in the park. There will be times when physically, mentally and emotionally you will be challenged, perhaps under duress. Psychologically, the cold shower is like a shield for you for the rest of the day. It is said that if you conquer the coldness of the water, you can conquer the chilliness of whatever life brings.

The cold water causes your capillaries to open, filling them with more blood, flushing out the toxins and all deposits. When they return to normal, the blood goes back to the organs, each with their own blood supply. The result is a stimulation of secretions of the glandular system, which are the guardians of your health. If your glandular system and blood chemistry are constantly being refreshed, your nervous system is strengthened and youthfulness is prolonged.

When I first learned about this process, I immediately said, "No way". I live in Chicago where it is cold enough! But saying "yes" to a new idea was an attitude I was beginning to cultivate, so I made a deal with myself. I would do it for a week. It has been over 5 years now that this has been part of my morning routine.

Taking the cold shower is a bit different from the typical rinse. First, rub your body with pure oil, like almond oil, which has a high mineral content. Then be careful not to get the top of your head or the tops of your thighs wet. The femur bone in the thigh controls the calcium-magnesium balance in your body. Move in and out of the water, as you let the cold water hit each part of your body. Massage each area until it starts to feel hot. Make sure you rotate so that you get all parts of your body. Don't forget your underarms. That is where some of your lymph nodes are located. The best way to get the legs is to use one foot to massage the other.

Start with 30 seconds (come on, you can do it, it's 30 seconds!). Work up to 1 or 2 minutes. As you towel dry, rub your body briskly. Often, to add to this experience, I chant as I shower. (It will keep you from screaming!)

(Note: A cold shower is not an appropriate In-sourcing exercise for pregnant and menstruating women; they should take warm showers)

WATER, WATER ...

What does drinking sufficient water every day have to do with inner happiness? Just as the body reacts to irregularities of the mind, the reverse is true. Without sufficient hydration even the most spiritual among us would find it difficult to focus on inner peace, the lack of ample fluids causing fuzzy thinking, fatigue, joint pain, or even headaches. Water is everywhere in our body. Our blood is 90% water; our total body weight is 70-75% water. It is clearly our body's most important nutrient. Yet often we do not take into account the body's need for hydration and wait until we are noticeably thirsty to drink the water needed.

The yogis say that water, along with air and fire, is one of the essential elements that keep us in balance and flow. Sufficient hydration aids in maintaining normal body temperature, metabolizes fat, aids in digestion, lubricates organs, and flushes toxins. The kidneys, sex glands, and the lymphatic system are the physical manifestations of the water element. Obviously (but often ignored), drinking water is necessary to keep the body functioning at its optimal level.

So drink up! At least 64 ounces of water a day is the minimum to keep our bodies humming along.

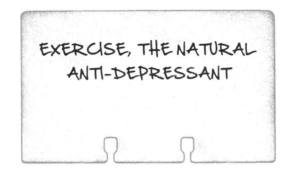

EXERCISE, THE NATURAL ANTI-DEPRESSANT

It's tiresome to be reminded how essential it is to set aside time each and every day for exercise. But the benefits simply can't be ignored. Exercise is one of the most effective anti-depressants we know of and considering the side effects associated with *Zoloft* and *Prozac* – dependency, risks of nausea, vomiting, fever, sleepiness, uneven heartbeat, confusion, fainting, seizures and danger of coma - my vote goes to the elliptical and treadmill machines and better yet, a long walk along the lake.

Frankly, much as I'd like to say otherwise, a casual approach to the discipline is not sufficient, you have to 'program' yourself to the task. For me the impetus comes from setting aside the same block of time every morning before breakfast. My husband prefers to put in his time after work. For me, exercise is energizing; for him, it's a chore. For both of us it's a fixed part of our daily routine. You don't have to train to run a marathon or climb Mount Everest; it doesn't even have to be a "work out" per se; just walk for thirty minutes or garden for an hour or join the kids in the playground. Consciously set aside time to do something! Your mood will improve because exercise generates a chemical reaction in your body, actually escalating your serotonin levels, which in turn, as medically authenticated, will increase positive thinking and a sense of emotional well being

But still we resist, making every excuse to avoid the trip to the gym. My recommendation is a yoga routine, especially Kundalini yoga. This version of yoga makes the connection between the body and the mind patently clear: change your body (chemistry) and you change your mind (mood) and subsequently, your behavior. With yoga, not only do you connect the body and the mind, you also connect to the spirit. By spirit, I mean you connect to your conscious awareness, to the energy flow of the universe through you.

THINK ABOUT WHAT YOU EAT

Let me assure you right off the bat, this is not a nag, nag, nag admonition threatening death from scurvy or morbid obesity lest you eat not a mouthful more than fifteen hundred calories a day and a bowl of fresh kale daily. Truth be known, I am a vegetarian who eats ribs!

What can I say? I enjoy ribs; even though I consciously know that eating a vegetarian diet is much better for me and the environment as well. But that said, every once in a while I decide to order up the baby backs despite the health negatives. It's a conscious choice I occasionally make after making sure I'm not kidding myself when I characterize the indulgence as a once-in-a-while treat. The point I'm making is, being sanctimonious about 'eating right' can turn a healthy lifestyle choice into a three-times-a-day chore that feels more like a sacrifice than an easily accomplished routine. What I'm asking you to do for the next forty days is purposely think about your menu choices before every breakfast, lunch and dinner. Don't make the decisions be about deprivation. Let common sense be your guide. Recognize that what you resist, persists! So when you feel tempted to have an ice cream, give yourself permission to have it, but consciously postpone the purchase "until later." Chances are, when 'later' comes, you'll find that you may not want that chocolate fudge cone with sprinkles!

Back to the risks we carnivores run; most of you know the many health related reasons for giving up meat. Not the least of which is, your life is prolonged. Vegetarians typically have lower cholesterol and blood pressure levels and live six to ten years longer on average due to fewer instances of the three biggest killers: heart disease, cancer and strokes. The reason for the decreased incidence of illness is documented: the blood is more alkaline when eating plant-based foods. Optimally, the blood should be 75% alkaline and 25% acidic.

Equally important are the numerous environmental reasons for minimizing the amount of meat in our diets. The deleterious effect of greenhouse gas emissions polluting the atmosphere is well publicized* as are the damages caused by land erosion and toxic water sources (760 tons of grain yearly are fed to farmed animals so that people can eat meat, not including an additional 100 tons used for biofuels). Raising animals for slaughter poses weighty philosophic concerns. Factory farms cram animals by the thousands into filthy windowless sheds, wire cages, gestation crates and other confinement systems. There is a spiritual component as well: *Ahimsa*, a yogic principle, means 'doing no harm.' If we see all living beings as being part of one consciousness, our connectedness would mean that harming an animal is like harming yourself.

*A recent United Nations report entitled *Livestock's Long Shadow* concludes that eating meat causes almost 40 per cent more greenhouse-gas emissions than all the cars, trucks, ships and planes in the world combined.

CONTROL YOUR BREATH -
CONTROL YOUR EMOTIONS

It's the critical last seconds of a NBA game. The star stands at the foul line to take the shot that will win the game, or lose it. The camera cuts to a close up of his face. He takes a deep breath, holds it for a moment then exhales with an explosive puff of air. It's a technique that athletes use to relax themselves at critical moments. And it works. The star sinks the shot and his team wins.

Breathing, the act of inhaling and exhaling is so fundamental to our existence we rarely think about it. We do it unconsciously. However, when we become aware of the breathing process, conscious of how we can control the flow of life-giving air into and out of our lungs, our sense of who we are - of life itself – can be expanded dramatically. With the game on the line, if you can control your breath, you can control your emotions.

With so many positive benefits associated with conscious breathing – lowered pulse rate; reduced levels of anxiety - it's curious to note that a great many people breathe incorrectly. All too often as I guide clients to the relaxed trance state that conscious breathing can create, I observe them inadvertently employing "reverse breathing" or "chest breathing," two unsound variations from the norm that are not optimal. (I, too, was a reverse breather, contracting rather than expanding my stomach when inhaling. After learning to breathe correctly, I noticed a definite increase in my ability to relax and deal effectively with my emotions).

Concentrate on inhaling through the nose. As you do so, put your hand on your belly button and imagine the belly as a big red balloon. As you inhale, fill the balloon by expanding your belly, allowing the inhaled air to fill your lower chest, then rising up as far as possible to fill your upper chest. Slowly exhale through the nose (not the mouth!). Imagine the balloon deflating little by little, first from the upper chest, then your lower chest, then your belly, pulling your belly button back so that it touches the small of your back. Continue doing this for 5 breaths.

Every day has some degree of anxiety waiting to ambush you. This is a quote from Thich Nhat Hanh that I recite to ease my agitation. "Breath is the bridge which connects life to consciousness, which unites your body to your thoughts."

TIME OUT FOR PLAY TIME

Recently I read that the amount of learning that takes place between birth and age six is greater than all the years accumulatively thereafter. Obviously the brain grows most rapidly during our toddler years. But more is at play than simply the growth of the brain. It's the nurturing energy that encourages the child to explore and experience without inhibition. Take a walk past a neighborhood playground filled with dozens of pre-school kids and you'll see the phenomenon in action. In psychological terms, this type of unfettered energy is known as 'right brain' or 'magnetic' (also referred to as 'moon' or feminine energy).

As we begin to "educate" our youngsters and introduce them to math and science the capacity for learning shifts to 'left brain' or 'laser' mode, (so-called 'sun' or 'masculine' energy). That's not a "bad" thing in of itself, but as tests and measurement of skills get emphasized, the tendency is to minimize the more uninhibited side of the process. Consequently, the desire to 'score high' can tilt the synchronicity of the right/left sides of the brain (despite the fact that it is the creative or playful right side that discovers what the left side presents as quantifiable, empirical data!)

And so we have the description of so many of us today—focusing on the measurable: salaries, our rung on the pecking order, winning rather than the joy of playing. We downplay and stifle our inner child's delight for fear that expressing it will cause embarrassment.

When it feels as if life has become a series of tasks rather than moments to enjoy, it's time to take time for yourself and to put the focus on the fun of what you're doing rather than the pressure of doing it 'right.' The experts in early childhood development know the value of taking frequent breaks from 'learning.' The recess you used to have in kindergarten days was for more than taking a nap; it provided opportunity for the right side of the brain to process and integrate what the left side absorbed. In the adult world opportunity for a snooze mid-way in the day rarely presents itself. But no matter how busy and hectic your schedule may be there is time for a respite from the chaos. Make use of it. Schedule it if you can; a few minutes before lunch; or better yet, before you leave for home (so you can leave your work at the office, where it should stay).

Repose after high-energy activity is essential for the body to restore itself. That's the purpose of *savasana*, or corpse pose, after the end of any yoga class – to integrate what the body has absorbed and convert the energy into wisdom. My trick when things get tense is to pause and conjure up in my mind a special beach I frequent when on vacation in Mexico. The sub-conscious doesn't know time or place, so I can 'go there' anytime I wish!

38

PAMPER YOURSELF

There are an alarming number of men and women who suffer from stress-related exhaustion from trying to cope with ever-longer work weeks, energy-draining commutes and the increasing demands of high pressure jobs... not to mention family responsibilities when the work day ends. The consequences go far beyond acting like a grouch when the kids are playing their music too loud. If stressful conditions continue too long the body starts to react: secretions from the adrenal glands increase; heart beat rates amplify; blood pressure rises. So it's physically as well as emotionally essential to avoid the crash lurking around the corner by putting on the brakes before careening out of control. Here is one of my favorite ways to avoid burn out when the world around me resounds with discord and strife.

I take a bath... more accurately, a deep soak that immerses the cells for at least 20-minutes in a blend of salt, hydrogen peroxide and tea (yes, tea), a recipe that seeps into the cells of the body where our emotional memories are stored energetically. As you sink into the fragrant hot bath, you can literally feel your level of stress diminish as the water sooths and nurtures you, releasing the cellular memories and restoring your inner serenity. Ahhhhh.

Here is the recipe that my dear colleague Cathy Chapman gave me for what I call the Love Yourself Bath.

1/3 cup of sea salt
1/3 cup of hydrogen peroxide
8 cups of chamomile tea (made by boiling 2 tea bags for 15 minutes)

Pour that mixture into a bathtub filled with water at a temperature that is comfortable enough so that you can stay in it for 20 minutes. Then, using a washcloth with no soap, massage each part of your body in a circular motion, telling each part, "I love you."

Of course, taking a Love Yourself Bath for forty consecutive days might be unrealistic! But the idea of pampering yourself on a daily basis is a practical way to ward off stress. Put aside a time that is yours and yours alone; do something to rejuvenate and create that "get away from it all" respite from the chaos of the day.

THE EXTRAORDINARY POWER OF LAUGHTER

Kathy Griffin, Chris Rock, Sarah Silverman... we know them as hilarious comedians – but according to a number of highly credible medical studies perhaps we should address them as "Laughter Doctors." It turns out that the venerable *Reader's Digest* was right when one of their more popular columns proclaimed, "Laughter is the Best Medicine." Over the past two decades serious medical studies have submitted credible evidence to support the therapeutic value of laughing. Recently a considerable amount of publicity has focused attention on "the Laughing Guru," an Indian doctor named Madan Kataria, who has created an entire yoga curriculum with laughing as the prescription for total well-being (estimates of the number of people who engage regularly in Kataria's exercises are as high as two hundred and fifty thousand).

One of the first and perhaps the most celebrated example of laughter's curative powers came from Norman Cousins, the famed editor of the *Saturday Review*. His 1979 best seller,

Anatomy of an Illness" described how laughing at the antics of the Marx Brothers contributed to his recovery from a painful degenerative disease of the joints that doctors had diagnosed as incurable. Several years later a psychiatrist from Stanford collaborated on an experiment to prove Cousins' contention, sampling the blood of a colleague watching episodes of "Laurel and Hardy" and "Abbott & Costello." Results of the study showed "measurable and significant neuro-endocrine and stress hormone changes with mirthful laugher." Since then and to the current day, dozens of subsequent reports maintain that laugher can have a salutary effect on everything from heart disease to diabetes and allergies.

In my waiting room I have a bulletin board overflowing with *New Yorker* cartoons. It's not unusual for clients to enter my office laughing after reading them. It's a good start to our session, a reminder that if we can laugh at ourselves we can look at our problems with a more positive and balanced perspective. Have you ever attended a wake or memorial for a loved one and listened to friends telling humorous stories about the deceased? The grief we feel is not extinguished but the focus is shifted – we celebrate life as well as accept the inevitable.

When asked what attributes are most important in a mate, I have found that lots of my clients list "sense of humor" in the top five. One of my husband's gifts to me when we got married was his promise to make me laugh every day. For the past 24 years he has kept his promise.

Laughter yoga (also known as *hasya yoga*) is becoming increasingly popular because it reinforces something children already know instinctively: that laughter makes you feel better. (It's estimated that kids laugh about 400 times a day, and adults only about 15). As developed by Doctor Kataria, there are many varieties of laughing exercises. We can try one right now: raise both arms in the sky with the head tilted a little backwards and laugh hardily for about thirty seconds. Do you feel more peaceful? There's evidence that a good, hearty laugh can actually relax your muscles for up to 45 minutes by triggering the release of endorphins, the body's natural, feel-good chemicals.

MIND

The power of positive thinking is a concept that has been documented and proved without dispute. When you shift the focus away from denigrating thoughts to those that bolster self-esteem you can change the way you feel about yourself and change the way you behave.

The following contemplations guide you to 'mindsets' that will enable you to generate the positive energy required for powering a life of joy and fulfillment.

LIVE IN THE NOW

I like this expression, "As long as you're here you might as well show up." What is the point of continuously allowing the events of the past to fill you with resentment or regret? You cannot change the past, there is no re-editing for a happier ending, what transpired is history. It's done, *finis, terminado, fertig,* no matter how you say it, it's in the can. Why would you like to re-live and suffer something you cannot do anything about? And what is the point of continuously thinking about what might happen in the future that might make your life better? You cannot predict the outcome of events before they take place. Remember the joke: "If you want to make God laugh, tell him your plans." Most of the things we fear don't happen, anyway. You have the life you are living now, at this precise moment in time.

Yet all too often we live in a state of regret for the past or anxiety for the future. It's understandable: we live in a crazy world that literally drives us to distraction 24/7 with a clamorous barrage of news, politics, gossip, social media, advertising, sports, cyber blogs, texts, tweets, junk mail and endless chatter about celebrity nonsense and impending apocalypse. When we're at work, we fantasize about being on vacation; on vacation, we worry about the work piling up on our desks. We get stuck on intrusive memories of the past or fret about what may or may not happen in the future. In doing so, we let the present slip away. Life unfolds in the present but we can't appreciate the here and now when we're trapped in thoughts of the future or the past. If we sip a latte and think, "This is not as good as what I had last week," or decide to have a scone and fret that they might run out of blueberry, we are not experiencing, let alone enjoying, what's happening right now.

Living in the moment makes people happier, not just at the moment they're savoring their coffee and scone, but enduringly, because typically our thoughts about the past and future are laced with negative energy. We think about the past and become awash in regret and remorse that things didn't turn out differently, or we become depressed wishing – fruitlessly of course - for things we don't have. We miss the rewards right in front of us because we are looking beyond the present to what once was or what might be. We think about the future and our brows furrow with worry anticipating the worst, troubled about things that haven't happened yet and might not happen at all. (I get a laugh from this Mark Twain quote, "I have known a great many troubles, but most of them never happened").

Remember the expression, "Go with the flow." It's good advice. It means more than simply paying attention to your surroundings. It means to live in the now, fully engaged in the present moment, your attention so focused that distractions cannot penetrate.

Going with "the flow" is more than philosophical counseling – it is instruction to be taken literally! It refers to the flow of your breath and consciously controlling inhalations and exhalations. Calmed by your measured breathing, you are mindful that certain things are beyond your control. You know that on occasion there will be events causing you sadness or stress or anger whether you like it or not. But it is pointless to relive them over and over again, or worry in vain that they will come to pass again. In the flow of life – the breath of life - you embrace your feelings as they are. To put it humorously, 'be here now, be someplace else later, is that so complicated?'

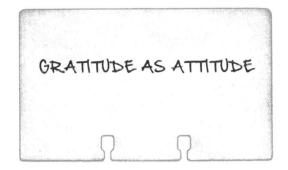

GRATITUDE AS ATTITUDE

Each morning as I am awakened by my alarm clock, as my consciousness is beginning to push its way up from sleep, I utter the words, "Thank you, I made it through the night. I am alive." Then, with that first deep breath of the dawning day, I make a mental list of everything for which I am grateful, not simply reciting the obvious — good health, loving family, fulfilling career — but visualizing and appreciating the small gifts as well as the awesome blessings that life has bestowed. (I remember one day when I got some dust in my eye, I couldn't see for a moment. Was I ever grateful that my blindness was only temporary! "How lucky I am to have my vision," I thought to myself.)

The positive energy of gratitude sets the tone for the day that follows. I set off feeling optimistic rather than pessimistic. Not surprisingly, the paybacks of affirmative energy go far beyond the philosophical. There are practical benefits. You'll be better able to overcome stress because thinking positively rather than negatively when dealing with frustrating events allows you to see solutions, not just problems. And with less stress, you gain extra pep to do the things you enjoy.

Mind you, the words that express gratitude mean nothing without the intention behind them. Watch a mother admonish her child to "Say thank you to the nice lady." The mumbled words are delivered simply to satisfy mom; they're more about being polite than grateful. True gratitude doesn't take the gift of life for granted, remembering always the impermanence of our time on earth, and the good fortune with which we have been blessed.

BE INSPIRED

Recently, it seemed like the whole world was reading *The Girl with the Dragon Tattoo*. When I started reading it, I couldn't put it down. However, after reading it I vowed not to read the other two books of the trilogy. In fact, I wanted to erase the images from my conscious awareness. It did nothing to make me feel happy.

How different I feel reading the words of his holiness the Dalai Lama or Thict Nat Hhan, or the poetry of Rumi or Wordsworth. For many years, Howard and I would read daily from Joan Borysenko's book, *Pocketful of Miracles*. It is a collection from all traditions of uplifting thoughts and behaviors for each day. I'm also reminded of a loving young mother who told me when her kids pull her off center, she opens Alfie Kohn's book, *Unconditional Parenting*. It doesn't matter to her where she opens it; inherent in the title it provides her with the inspiration she needs to regain her stability

The same could be true of listening to music. The body reacts so differently to the harsh notes of heavy metal then to the melodies of Beethoven.

Don't misunderstand me, I enjoy the thrills of a good story or the rhythms of modern music or the fantasy of a new movie, but there is a difference between scraping the surface for thrills and going deeper to find the core of inspiration. It takes some digging to get beneath the facade, deeper than the superficial and superfluous. The exploration of the inner Self, where true happiness is found, is worth the effort. The intention is to thrive not just survive.

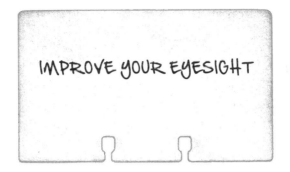

IMPROVE YOUR EYESIGHT

When my parents retired they bought a condominium in Hollywood, Florida across the street from the beach. It was as close to the stunning ocean view that they could afford, they explained; the more luxurious skyscrapers directly on the shoreline being too costly for their limited savings. When I visited them they used to say, "Let's get up early and go across the street to see the sun rise." My unspoken response at the time was, "Why didn't you save enough money to buy a place on the beach?" To me, their investment was "close but no cigar," as we packed our blankets and hiked through the parking lots, dodged traffic and sneaked across the manicured gardens of the expensive condominiums before arriving at the public beach. Rather than being inspired by the view I felt shamed by what I construed to be the humiliating journey there.

Years later my husband and I bought a townhouse in Ixtapa, Mexico about fifteen minutes from the beach. It was as close to the magnificent ocean view as we could afford, the more luxurious sky-rises directly on the shoreline being too costly for our limited savings. Once or twice a week while there, we pack our blankets and make our way across the next-door golf course, hike up a steep section of the town's thoroughfare and climb a cobble stone path to a beautiful bay on the outskirts of town noteworthy for a beach un-paralleled for its charm. We arrive, tired but exhilarated and inspired by the view, as if seeing it for the first time.

What had changed? What had transformed essentially the same journey from a humiliating slog into an enjoyable hike?

The answer becomes clear as we make our life's journey from childhood to our "wisdom years." Along the way we learn to transcend the ego, to dip into our real natures, to open up to who we are... and to see the miracle of nature with increased clarity, even as our eyesight grows dim. It is the way you look at the world that determines how the world appears for you. And inevitably, as we grow older (and wiser) the expansion of our understanding and awareness of a divine, universal Oneness enables us to see past the disarray of a world in turmoil. When you have a strong foundation of spiritual self-respect, you aren't as easily swayed by the judgments of others or prone to equate material acquisitions with happiness. When we take our ego out of the equation, our inner and external selves merge, and our capacity to appreciate life blossoms.

Simply put, in Mexico we made a conscious choice to see the beauty that was right in front of our eyes. We had learned to re-frame circumstances to see the good inherent in all things.

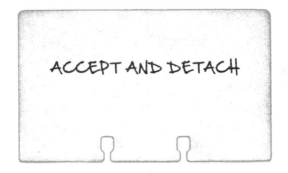

ACCEPT AND DETACH

God give me the courage to change the things I can,
The serenity to accept the things I can't,
And the wisdom to know the difference.

Reinhold Niebuhr, "The Serenity Prayer"

Midway during a particularly difficult Yoga session I faltered, my muscles protesting, several minutes remaining before the exercise was completed. I thought to myself, "I'm going to stop, this is too hard." My teacher smiled at me and said, "Don't listen to your mind." Then she added, sounding like an ad for *Nike*, "Just do it, your mind is not your master."

Being sports minded, I understood the physical implication. Marathon runners, for example, hit the wall but continue on, ignoring the protests from their aching muscles and in effect, shutting off communication with the mind. But what about the application to the emotional pain suffered in everyday life? There are many times during the day when the world is too much with us. Stuck in a grid locked traffic jam or up to our ears in pressing paperwork, the stress can be overwhelming. On those occasions, slowly succumbing to a state of duress, how do we tell the anguished mind, "You're not the boss of me"? At those times, how do we press on, persevering in the face of emotional pain that prompts the mind to shriek, "Enough already."

You can start by losing the "woe is me" attitude. You relinquish your power when you give in to feeling that you're a victim. Instead, substitute the wise words of Deepak Chopra, "accept the present and intend the future." The more you focus on pain, the more it persists. As the saying goes, "What you resist, persists." Only when you completely accept the situation as it is, can the situation change. This means, paradoxically, that the way to eliminate pain is to not try to eliminate it. Accept your feelings of angst, acknowledge the pain, and then move through the anguish into the present moment. It may sound simplistic, but you *can* choose to feel better!

It's normal from time to time for pain to be part of your life. Learn to accept it and to detach yourself from the hurt it might be causing you. It's pointless to waste your time and energy wishing and hoping that things will be different. There is a saying that goes, "The ties that bind you shall set you free." The more you struggle against the unpleasant circumstances of the present moment, the more time and energy you waste. Accept and detach. Use the surfing technique. Be in the present moment. When you trust that good things are coming, they have a way of showing up!

(NON) JUDGMENT DAY

White Tantric Yoga is a daylong, couple's meditation retreat taught by the Kundalini Research Institute. It's held once a year in Chicago and as a purifying technique, it is extremely powerful. For my first experience of it my husband was unable to attend, so I arrived alone. During the morning session I was paired up with one of my yoga buddies from class so performing the somewhat intimate gestures wasn't awkward. But before the afternoon classes were scheduled to begin, she had to leave. Imagine the room with about 50 pairs of people all in pristine white, facing each other in close proximity. As I waited for my new partner my anxiety was palpable. Minutes before the session's opening meditation a portly man sat down in front of me, wearing black! I couldn't stifle my initial reaction; he was creepy. Many of the meditations had us literally eye-to-eye, head to head, in each other's space for 31 to 62 minutes at a time. The anxieties I felt didn't abate... until I looked up to see the words of Yogi Bhajan printed on the wall in front of me: "If you can't see God in all, you can't see God at all." By the time the afternoon was over my partner and I hugged, sincerely thanking each other for our experience together. The lesson of "I am that, too" was made very clear to me. As the expression goes, "You spot it, you got it."

Most judgements we make about others are based on stereotypes. We give people labels and pigeonhole them. By putting them down we prop ourselves up in order to feel superior. We lapse into an "us and them" mentality where "they" always manage to come out beneath the "us." It doesn't serve us well. It creates a divide between people and restricts our interactions because we fail to make an effort to get to know or understand others. Conversely, the benefits of being non-judgmental are many. When we leave the negative garbage in the dumpster gentleness takes over. We find ourselves substituting open-minded curiosity for premature conclusions and in the process uncovering commonalities and shared experiences. Everyone has a backstory. When we offer a nonjudgmental ear to listen to it, we can understand a person for who he is rather than jumping to conclusions based on how they look or the peculiarities they may present.

THE "GOOD" GOOD-BYE

When something or someone has been part of your life for as long as you can remember, it's not easy to say good-bye. That's understandable when it's time to say farewell to the home where you grew up or to a loved one that has passed. But often the reluctance to say good-bye to some experience or relationship that is *not* good for us, is equally or even more difficult.

It's helpful to first examine the association and then detach from it. For example, when I help a client stop smoking, part of the process is to say goodbye to the last pack of cigarettes. I ask the person to think of the significance behind the smoking. For some the cigarette was regarded as a friend to turn to when they were lonely; for others, it was a comfort when they felt anxious. Now the task is clear - to search for and find healthier choices to satisfy the role played by smoking and to replace the cigarette poison with a better option.

Let's apply that process to a relationship or link to the past that doesn't serve you well.

A familiar scenario I often see involves mothers and fathers and their grown sons and daughters. Typically, poor decisions made in the past, when the parents were immature and perhaps self absorbed with career and personal unrest, have become rooted in memory where they unendingly trigger remorse and regret. I suggest that there is no value to reliving the events of the past, assigning blame and/or holding on to grief and anger. The subconscious does not differentiate past, present and future. Forgiving loved ones for transgressions of the past will have a direct impact on your relationships in the present and future. Lessons learned are more important than continually reliving the pain. When that understanding sinks in, and the old wounds are healed and the old transgressions are shed and you finally forgive yourself and others, you can say goodbye and move on, *emerging* into the present and committing to a new way of interacting with the relationships you have changed profoundly.

FORGIVE... AND FLOURISH

There is a saying that goes, "Holding on to anger is like drinking poison and expecting the other person to die." So why is it so hard to forgive?

Perhaps because forgiveness can be confused with condoning what someone has done to us. Forgiveness is not an accepting or pardoning of a horrific act, nor does it suggest you are weak if you choose to forgive. Forgiveness doesn't deny the other person's responsibility for hurting you, and it doesn't minimize or justify the wrong. Forgiveness need not require reconciliation; you can forgive the person without excusing the act.

The reason to forgive is to free yourself of locked-in negative energy, replacing it with a kind of peace that helps you go on with life.

Nearly everyone has been hurt by the actions or words of another. Perhaps your mother criticized your parenting skills or your partner had an affair. These wounds can leave you with lasting feelings of anger, bitterness and even vengeance — but if you don't practice forgiveness, you may be the one who pays most dearly by bringing anger and bitterness into every relationship and new experience. Your life may become so wrapped up in the wrong of the past that you can't enjoy the present. There is a physical price as well. Holding on to anger and resentment can trigger high levels of the stress hormone, cortisol, and have an adverse effect on your cardiovascular, muscular-skeletal and immune systems.

By embracing forgiveness, you embrace peace, hope, gratitude and joy. Forgiveness does not change the past, but it enables our *feelings* about the past to change. We can be complete with what was previously unresolved, and move on; accepting that whatever happened is history. Now we are free to enjoy a healthier, happier life, living in the present, in the now. When you let go of grudges, you'll no longer define your life by how you've been hurt.

And just as there are adverse health symptoms from holding on to a grudge, there are positive health benefits from letting it go. If we open our hearts, we can proactively access empathy and love, which will trigger secretion of the positive hormone, serotonin. It's been proven that reduction in depressive symptoms can lead to improved sleep quality, reduced fatigue and somatic complaints and a strengthened spirituality.

I know that confronting hatred and loss with an open heart is extremely difficult, but isn't it worth trying instead of poisoning yourself? Scan your psyche and find a wound that still bleeds. Hold the event at arm's length, observing it rather than being caught up in it. Be understanding rather than judgmental... and forgive the person(s) who hurt you.

Forgive me if I may have left the most important point for last. For the hurt you may have inflicted on others, forgive yourself. Sometimes your most sincere and heartfelt apology will not be accepted. The regret you express so passionately may be ignored. Your earnest offer to make amends may be greeted with disdain. Let it go if there is nothing more that you can do: forgive yourself. Otherwise, you will remain engaged in a relentless, daily battle of futility.

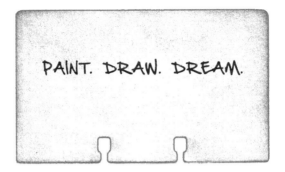

PAINT. DRAW. DREAM.

I took an adult education watercolor class a few years back. It was the first time I had ever had any art instruction, and I was in my late 50's at the time! Most of my fellow students had previously explored their inner artist and after observing their work I admit to having had talent envy. Nevertheless, I kept painting.

Many lessons later, even though I had not advanced to a level where I'd show my work to anyone, I felt accomplished. A new world had opened and I was absorbed into it. As I walked about the city I noticed the shades of color and wondered what mix of paints would match them. I saw shapes and perspectives and imagined how I'd illustrate them. Even mundane images became alive as I saw them through my "artist's eyes." I remember, in particular, one drab, January morning walking to work through the neighborhood park. Everything was gray and the "same." Except it wasn't! One red leaf still remained on the bare branches of a Maple tree.

It leapt out at me... and led me to a contemplation of nature that lifted my spirits high.

Today, although I no longer pick up the brushes as frequently as I would like, the insights I gained from my painting lessons remain present. Quite simply, I look at the marvels of nature with an altered perception. And the pictures in my mind are exquisite!

In this frenetic world it is 'normal' to rely heavily on the left, or rational, brain. But it is important to balance your practical side with your creative side, and painting – regardless of the medium – is a delightful hobby to pursue. You'll be astounded how picturing a scene on your easel can translate into new and unique ways of solving problems at work and home.

MEAN WHAT YOU SAY

Do you recall the wedding vows you made as you stood in front of the dais and promised to love your spouse till death do you part? If you're single, can you bring to mind a life-affirming commitment to a family member or true blue friend? Can you evoke the depth of your feelings... how you were immersed into the moment, totally absorbed into the pledge you made?

Inevitably, time and familiarity reduce the intensity of our vows. Our ardent "I love you" becomes a "love ya" afterthought before we hang up the phone and return to the business at hand. That's the problem with commitments: they're easier to make than to keep. And when it's all talk and no walk the result is the opposite of what is intended. Instead of the soaring spirit that comes from fulfillment and a resolute integrity, an incipient feeling of guilt seeps into your consciousness and gets buried with a shrug, "It's okay, I meant well."

A true commitment is not some grandiose promise that makes you feel good at the time but in reality is all puff and bluster. "I'm going to lose weight," "I'm going to tell my mother I love her," "I'm going to get a better job," are well-intended commitments, but lack teeth and power. Contrast the words of two participants at a Self Fulfillment workshop I attended. The first person stood up, all aglow with fervor, and from the bottom of his heart pledged to end hunger in the world. The second person was shy and humble. "I work in a pizza parlor and I promise to make the best pizza I can for each and every customer I serve." Each avowal rang with sincerity but one was all about the words and the other was all about the will.

I have a simple guideline to follow when making a commitment, an acronym that helps me gauge if my declaration is real or bogus. I put it to the PMS test, asking myself if my commitment is Precise, Measurable and Specific. It also helps to start your commitment with the words, "I will," as in "I will finish a draft of this handbook by the end of 2012." It adds power to the promise. And speak it out loud! Actually say the words to someone who can hold you to what you've committed to, because being heard is what 'puts it out there,' into the universe where its existence is affirmed.

Actually, let me refine what I just said. Instead of saying "I will," make your declaration in the first person, present tense: "I finish the draft by the end of 2012." Since the subconscious mind does not know the difference between past, present and future, now you are attracting the energy to the statement as if it has already happened. And then it does!

LESS FACEBOOK - MORE FACE TO FACE

Recently I read an article in the *New Yorker* about a class NYU is giving to incoming freshmen on "How to Talk to Each Other in Person." I was stunned. It seems that young people have become so accustomed to meeting through Facebook and communicating by using emails, tweets and texting, they no longer know how to connect face to face.

Technology links people together but disconnects the essential elements of a relationship. Baud speed and multiple access are not replacements for intimacy and thoughtfulness. When I watch a distracted rider on the "L" idly thumbing a text message to someone in cyberspace it's clear to me the gadgetry matters more than the words being said. Pedestrians talking on their cell phones as they stroll down Michigan Avenue are trivializing the essential importance of time and distance. How disturbing! I can still remember my mother talking on the wall mounted Bell telephone to her sister in New Jersey, exclaiming in an awed voice, "Fifty miles from the Bronx and I can hear her like she was in the same room. Imagine!"

Are we forgetting the art of personal and group inter-action? Let's hope not! Sharing feelings and spontaneous notions and unconfined reactions and the subtle meanings of unspoken words can deepen our understanding of others and strengthen our relationships. When I was growing up as a kid we didn't have cell phones and satellites and Global Positioning Systems and yet I knew most everybody in the neighborhood and they knew me. I never felt isolated or stranded high and dry, and I'm pretty certain my mother always knew where I went after school.

Of course so much of our busy day requires only a per-functory nod here, a casual hello/goodbye there. But along the way, try this: stop your pell mell rush from point A to point B and take time for a meaningful interchange of ideas and feelings shared among established and new found friends. Call a friend instead of texting and don't put off that date for coffee or lunch with a family member or friend you haven't seen in a while.

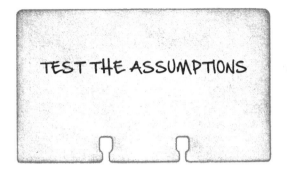

TEST THE ASSUMPTIONS

A prominent financier shows up at an important business meeting wearing a kilt. At first, the response of the bankers is disquieting. How should they respond? Do they approve the loan he has asked for? Why wouldn't they if the figures presented show positive returns? The prestige of the firm he represents hasn't changed. Nothing has changed — except the unexpected appearance of the kilt in lieu of a traditional suit.

My yoga teachers dress in traditional white clothing, wearing turbans. Children in my condo wear gray and blue uniforms to school. It is not shocking when women on the bus are wearing hijabs. On a hot summer day, it is common to see men and women in the skimpiest of outfits, shorts and halter-tops.

What assumptions do we make about outward appearances? How do others view us when our wardrobe strays from the "norm."? And most importantly, how do the assumptions made about you based on your outward appearance correlate to the inner persona, your true self?

Changing your "look" can be a fascinating exercise and lead you to a profound understanding of the importance of not allowing yourself to be swayed by appearances and the reactionary social judgments they evoke. As Saint Augustine observed, "If you only take into account the outer self, the only difference between human beings and beasts is that humans stand upright."

Conduct an experiment. Change your "look." If you are known for your preppy style, give *Izod* a rest and try on *Betsy Johnson*. If you are in a Johnny Cash stage and wearing only black, next time you go out wear white. Notice how you feel. Notice how you are treated. Are you being judged by your actions or your appearance? Very quickly it will become clear that one's value is not always obvious from what is seen on the surface. It's an important lesson, before we can accurately judge someone we need to take a deeper, closer look under the surface. Remember, as the saying goes, we can't judge a book by its cover.

CLEAN YOUR CLOSET,
AND SPEAK YOUR TRUTH

By itself, a messy closet doesn't qualify as a character flaw. But when you leave unnecessary "stuff" lying around, the clutter that's not properly put away gets in the way. And often is an external expression of your inner life.

Consider the correlation. As you sort through your clothes and shoes and accessories you'll find items you haven't worn for years: things you've outgrown; others long out of style. Similarly, as you review the *modus operandi* that manages your life, you'll find old, unbecoming habits that have accumulated: behavior mechanisms that portray you as victim; a facility at telling "white lies" that chip away at your integrity (Sorry I'm late, the traffic was bad... the battery in my phone went dead... my cat got sick).

Now recall the feeling that sweeps over you when the chore that has been hanging around for longer than it should, is completed. Not only is there more room in your neat closet, the nagging guilt that weighed heavier on you with each postponement, is dissipated. There's more room in your closet and more room for you to do the things you want to do. Again, the correlation: when your integrity is "all in" there's nothing to squirm about when you're interacting with loved ones or reporting to your boss or presenting to your professor. Without clutter you're open-minded and openhearted because there's no mess to step over and kick to the side. You can be true to who you really are.

We carry scraps of our past history hidden in layers of shame and rationalization. Unexposed, the behavior we have buried takes on a life of its own and becomes a distorted description of who you think you are. But whereas we can't change what happened in the past we can change our perception of ourselves by airing out the secrets that haunted us, and forgiving ourselves. You come to realize that who you are now is the person who will be recognized and accepted. You will be living your *Sat Nam*, what the yogis say to one another, "My name is truth. Truth is my identity."

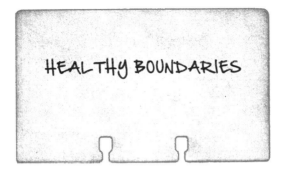

HEALTHY BOUNDARIES

The saying, "Good fences make good neighbors," doesn't suggest withdrawal from interacting with others, rather it serves as a reminder that setting healthy boundaries is essential to one's own happiness.

When there are no boundaries there is no differentiation between "you" and "me." If you are sad, so am I. If I am angry with someone, the expectation is you will be angry with the same person as well. It is merging as distinct from interacting. And if the merging is incomplete, there is a feeling of great loss.

When there are rigid boundaries, nothing is allowed in or out. Think about a country like North Korea where little information is allowed to flow in either direction. A particularly difficult dynamic occurs when a family has no boundaries within its structure yet rigid boundaries with the rest of the community.

A healthy boundary with respect to interpersonal relationships is permeable - allowing in the positive energy and keeping out the negative influences. The result is feeling whole and complete, interconnected rather than codependent. My trick is to visualize being surrounded by a golden net as I interact with people in my life. I allow the net to catch all negativity so I can assess it before reacting. I let in the positive interactions that support and value me.

CHILDHOOD DUES

The truth about our childhood is stored up in our body, and although we can repress it, we can never alter it. Our intellect can be deceived, our feelings manipulated, our perceptions confused, and our body tricked with medication. But someday the body will present its bill, for it is as incorruptible as a child, who, still whole in spirit, will accept no compromises or excuses, and it will not stop tormenting us until we stop evading the truth. **Alice Miller**

My experience as a psychotherapist validates this quote. The wounds of the past continue to plague us in many ways. Since thoughts, feelings and behaviors are all inter-connected, then the impact of our childhood lasts until we release the energy of events that have occurred. The body holds the imprints as physical pain and/or negative beliefs about oneself.

When I was a child, voicing my needs had little impact on my parents. Usually, the only time they provided uncon-ditional time and attention was then I was sick...and I was sick frequently, most often with tonsillitis. I wasn't heard, so why bother to speak. All the energy of hurt and frustration found a home in my throat, blocking energy, causing pain and illness.

Louise Hay, in *You Can Heal Your Life*, has a chart that illustrates the probable emotional reason for a number of illnesses. She also includes an antidote, a new positive thought pattern to shift the energy and change the direction to new feelings and behaviors.

Creating our own affirmations, our own new positive thought patterns, is even more powerful. If you see the connective bridge from today's difficulties through the feelings and thoughts, you can build a new bridge taking you to a new set of behaviors. As Alice Miller pointed out, unless you face your truth, the pain will continue.

At the end of the handbook there is Visualization for replacing the negative operating system with the positive. Do it as you meditate and afterwards, notice how different you feel and how your behaviors change.

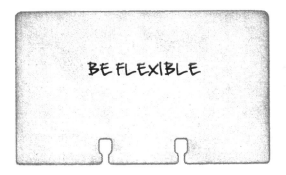

BE FLEXIBLE

When we have no control of our external world, we need to be flexible. Even the sturdiest foundations require flexibility. When living in the John Hancock building, I remember how surprised I was the first time I felt it swaying. The building cannot withstand the winds of the city without the flexibility built into the structure. The wise architects and engineers knew how rapidly the Chicago weather would change. And of course there is the fable about the willow and the oak tree...

Similarly, we too, cannot withstand the winds of change in our lives without built-in flexibility. It seems that life is always scuttling Plan A, causing us to hastily assemble Plan B. Without a plan B, or C, or D, as the case may be, we might snap when events beyond our control happen in our lives.

The trick to being flexible is to consciously stay focused on the intention, the end toward which your effort is directed, rather than the means to get there. It is the strength of your resolve to achieve your stated intention that allows you to adapt to new and unexpected circumstances and employ the resources we can control rather than be buffaloed by what is beyond our influence

Right from the start, be clear about your intention. Then make your plan(s) to achieve your aspiration. If the goal you set for yourself is seeded deep in unyielding resolve, the path to the desired end may inexplicably twist and turn along the way but you will not be deterred from success. I'm familiar with a young woman who was determined to become a teacher. Her plan was to go to a university out of town on a scholarship and study childhood education. Unfortunately her mother fell ill. Instead of college, she had to go to work to help support the family. Undeterred, she took evening classes at a local community college, then a nearby four-year school. Her plans changed, but her intention to become a teacher – and resolve to achieve her goal – was unwavering.

Intentions are not always as lofty as the example above. Every day we set uncomplicated objectives: "I'm going to work out this afternoon, I'm going to talk to the boss about a raise, I'm going to write a letter to my friend in the army." But grand or mundane, the impact on your psyche when the goal is achieved is remarkably satisfying. You feel good about yourself, fulfilled, your confidence is enhanced, and your self-esteem gets a healthy boost because your integrity is intact. You reaffirmed that you are not a victim of circumstance. You said you would do something, and you did it!

HELP SOMEONE HELP HIMSELF

Before I went into private practice I worked at a social service agency called Jewish Family and Community Service of Chicago. A number of my clients had significant money challenges and one of the services offered was to assist them financially. Being a new social worker, I thought "how easy! Someone needs money this month to pay the rent and to help them all I have to do is give them the money."

"Not so fast," said my wise supervisor. "Before you pay this month's rent, what is the plan for next month? Are you just delaying the inevitable?"

I soon learned the difference between rescuing someone and helping someone help himself. When I engaged the client in the process and found out the underlying reasons for the problem, I was able to guide him or her to see our donation as temporary help and then we could explore long-term solutions that were all-important to the big picture. To help someone help themselves is very empowering; it does not keep the person a victim but rather an active participant in their continued development.

So how does this bring you inner happiness? "If I rescue someone isn't that a good thing?" you may ask. Not necessarily. Rescuers are as much a "victim" as the perceived victim. If as a rescuer you get ego satisfaction only from "giving", then you will always need a victim to feel good about yourself, and you will become a victim of your own perceived generosity.

Helping someone help himself is more in balance. Giving and receiving brings equilibrium to the process. Imagine breathing as a metaphor for giving/receiving and try to just inhale without exhaling - you can't! You need a balance of both.

RECEIVING IS A
VITAL PART OF GIVING

You've heard the expression, "It's better to give than receive."
I think a more accurate statement is "It's easier to give than
receive."

I've witnessed this phenomenon many times at the conclusion of retreats and workshops where the participants
perform a ritual to honor their relationships by forming a
circle and taking turns washing each other's feet. You would
think that being pampered with a delightful sensation of
having the feet stroked and bathed with scented water
would leave you giggling with pleasure, but in most cases,
the opposite is true! The discomfort felt by those getting
their feet washed was palpable – they literally couldn't allow
themselves to sit back and enjoy the gift with which they
were being honored. Yet they participated fully and enthu-
siastically when it was their turn to be on their knees gently
bathing and kneading the feet of their partner.

There is a connection between this inability to receive
what essentially is a gift of love, and our unconscious

self-rejection of that part of us that seeks and is nurtured by intimate relationships. I've observed the source of this self-rejection many times during hypnotherapy sessions, when clients act out an event where parental disapproval of a perfectly natural and loving childhood sensation or impulse left behind lasting feelings of terror whenever similar sensations made themselves felt. The lesson learned: better to shut them down than run the risk of being scolded.

The consequence is not restricted to the wounded child/adult. Receiving is a necessary component of giving! Not as a *quid pro quo*, but as Yin to Yang, the balancing of your capacity to enlarge your sense of Self and your ability to empower others by the sharing that ensues.

WHISTLE A HAPPY TUNE

Perhaps you are too young to remember the 1951 Rogers and Hammerstein musical, *The King and I.* It was based on the story of *Anna and the King of Siam.* Did Rogers and Hammerstein have an awareness of 'mantra' when they wrote one of the songs, "Whistle a Happy Tune."? Mantra, an Eastern tradition, is really what this song is talking about.

Simply stated, mantra means *train the mind.* Remember, thoughts effect feelings and feelings effect behavior. So if you can shift a negative thought to a positive one, you will feel calmer, more in control and thus achieve a happier result.

Usually mantras are simple, short and have positive energy associated with its universal truth. It doesn't matter what language it is in, it is the intent of the words that is most important. Its power comes from the directness and repetition of the message. The mantra most associated with Kundalini Yoga is *Sat Nam*, which translates to mean "Truth is my name, my identity." When I find my mind wandering during meditation, I re-focus my attention by saying *Sat* on my inhalation and *Nam* on my exhalation.

When you find yourself with negative thoughts—"I can't do that"—say the opposite instead. Make a personal mantra for yourself: *I can do it!* Yogi Bhajan, the teacher who brought Kundalini Yoga to the western world, said, "God is everywhere, waiting for you to call. His zip code is His mantra."

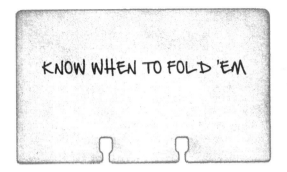

KNOW WHEN TO FOLD 'EM

Before we leave this section on how and where to find inner happiness within the Mind, consider this caution. Just as you would be careful when driving a vehicle, be careful of blindly committing to something or someone. Staying present and observing what is happening in this moment is essential.

If you are committed to running a marathon, for example, and you are feeling severe pain in the middle of the race, stop! If you are committed to a marriage and your spouse is unresponsive and abusive, get out! If you are following a spiritual teacher blindly, leave! Your most important commitment is to your highest self. If the assessment you make while in the present moment concludes that the pain is greater than the reward, trust yourself to make the necessary adjustments.

SPIRIT

Do not doubt the existence of the spirit! It lives within you, as a subtle body that illuminates what otherwise would be a bleak and joyless life. The following insights will guide you into the light when the unexpected changes of life require access to the open heart.

BLESSINGS

I have a friend who ends her letters and emails, not with Yours Truly or Sincerely, but with 'Blessings.' The closing pops out at me. It reminds me of the spiritual nature of my friend and imparts to me a sense of the sacred into an otherwise mundane day. It's a powerful word, instantly creating mindfulness of the inner realm and an appreciation of my comfortable life in the material world. I get the feeling that something good is coming my way!

Giving a blessing is more than the perfunctory acknowledgement of someone's sneeze. When given with true intention it's the bestowal of a divine gift, a reminder to turn inward and feel gratitude for your good fortune. To bless means to wish unrestricted good for others without the customary *quid pro quo*; it takes your connection to a higher rung.

Many of us have grown accustomed to a way of thinking that concludes we deserve all that we have been given. It's a point of view that ignores the most glorious blessing of all – the gift of life. And when we accept the reality that life is finite we recognize the impermanence of all things and understand, in that context, we don't own anything. So the blessing at the close of a letter or in response to a sneeze is a reminder of how dear the gift of life is.

It is so easy to become distracted and to forget one's true identity, particularly when grandiosity and similar ego-driven feelings make themselves felt. Take a few minutes each day to be mindful of your blessings and send them out into the world!

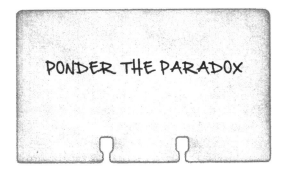

PONDER THE PARADOX

All things are impermanent. Yet you cannot destroy energy. How is that for a paradox? For me, rather than being a quizzical provocation, the contradiction is the key to genuine inner happiness. Let me explain in both spiritual and physical terms.

One of the most moving examples of impermanence was watching several Buddhist monks make one of their beautiful sand paintings, called a Mandela. It was during several summer days in Aspen, Colorado, where I was vacationing. Each afternoon I would check on their progress as they painstakingly constructed their masterpiece. Upon completion, they led a procession down to the river, carrying this delicate and artistic Mandela. After saying some prayers, they let it go to be subsumed by the rushing water. Imagine, after hours and hours of intricate, demanding labor, they destroyed their masterpiece in a matter of seconds!

Why on earth would they spend so much time creating a beautiful work of art only to let it melt away? Think of it in this way... isn't that what we all do, living our lives, hopefully with creativity and awareness, until the time we are absorbed back into whence we came?

If the spiritual aspect of the paradox is subjective, the other part of the incongruity is a physical reality: energy cannot be destroyed. Thus, the sand painting became a part of the river, whose water evaporated into the air, turning into clouds which rained back on the earth, feeding the plants and animals...and so on and so on.

We, too, leave our bodies to merge into the earth becoming a part of the never-ending cycle of life. Thus, the impact of the sand painting stays with me, as does the impact of the people who have left my life. This perception of 'the continuum of all things' goes beyond the philosophical. It's helpful on a daily basis as well. It is more productive and noticeably easier to glide through the day when the energy of our thoughts and feelings is positive rather than negative. When we stay conscious of life's complex paradox, we don't get so hooked on the either/or outcome of our endeavors. We can enjoy the highs without histrionics and bear the lows without sinking into depression being aware of the ultimate outcome in the greater scheme of things. (It's impossible to hold on to your ego and any sense of self-importance when watching the Mandela float away!)

List everything in your life that "never changes." If you think you've found something, look again to see how it does really change. List everything in your life that has been "destroyed." Again, if you can really find something that no longer exists, look again and notice the energy of your memories/ feelings/ thoughts.

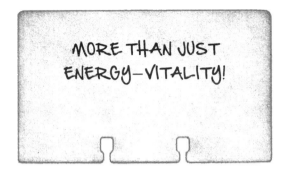

MORE THAN JUST ENERGY-VITALITY!

We are familiar with the benefits of working out regularly... jogging and lifting weights to increase our stamina and energy. The routine unquestionably pays us back for our effort, but like most of us, when we are finished exercising our muscles and expanding our cardiovascular endurance we simply shower and call it a day... leaving out what can be the most important part of the work out – the few minutes it takes to expand and convert the physical energy into a positive spiritual force... *vitality*.

As I am getting older, I am becoming more aware of the meaning of vitality. I used to think that having a lot of energy to get through the day was all I needed to feel complete. But something felt missing. Pushing through life wasn't enough. I felt out of harmony, but didn't know what it was I lacked. Now I know what it was. My energy levels were confined to my physical body but I lacked a revitalized (re-*vital*-ized) mind and spirit - vitality!

Here's the difference. Energy is what fuels you to do routine tasks. Vitality has to do with your ability to live — "vital" meaning "necessary to life." In broad terms, think of energy as a fuel for the body and vitality as 'soul power.'

On many levels, vitality is more important – and more elusive to build - than energy. If you are a tired woman or man, you can quickly increase your level of energy through exercise and healthy food choices. Gaining vitality requires responding to life with an unequivocal "spark," a kind of *joie a vive* that shows up as cheerfulness, enthusiasm and optimism. It is a prime ingredient for a high quality life.

The workout is not over when the weights are put away. It's important to 'exercise' the spiritual body as well as the physical. Add a two-minute 'vitality-rep' to your cool down by sitting on a bench in the locker room with the soles of your feet flat on the floor and your back straight. Close your eyes and visualize the energy created from the exercise session as a crackling, electrical force distributed to the muscles, organs, brain and heart. Feel the cells, the nerve endings, become alive and breathe deeply, oxygenating the blood stream. On the screen of your closed eyelids watch yourself become a conscious, sentient being, literally aglow with an aura of vitality.

MARVEL AT THE MIRACLES

It can happen when you least expect it: more than the scent of a rose bush in your garden; more than the rainbow after a summer shower. Perhaps you will notice out of the corner of your eye as you step out of the car parked on your gravel driveway, a tiny berry... cookie crumb... fragment of a leaf... moving along the ground. Idly, you look closer. It appears as if a large segment of the drive is swarming with moving seedpods! Perhaps they are from the Locust tree in your garden, but how could that be, the tree is fully fifty feet from the carport. You stoop lower to see the phenomenon more clearly. And you are stunned. Hundreds... thousands of carpenter ants are carrying seedpods literally two, three times their size and weight. It is as if the pyramids are to be built in a day. The imagination cannot translate the feat into human terms!

On vacation in Mexico, walking to the bus stop along a crumbling pavement, I heard a slight whirring in the air close by. I was passing a scraggly tree, nondescript, no different from the others lining the side of the walk, when suddenly, the branches exploded! Their golden bellies glistening like doubloons, a massive swarm of thumb-sized birds disappeared into the sky, their wings beating the air three feet from my awed eyes.

Again in Mexico, along its enchanted Pacific coast, a sudden movement just outside the breakers. I could have waded out to pet them on their bubble-nosed spouts - four dolphins, two adults and two babies, surfing the shallow waves. I swear I heard them laughing.

In New Zealand, along the gnarly coastline of the Northern Island, a herd of seals, hundreds of families, playing in the surf, sliding down drenched rock chutes as kids do at a water park. In Nova Scotia, about thirty miles from Halifax, a small town where we are directed to a barn yard and told to wait by the side of a crumbling out-building, only its unusually tall chimney still intact, opening to the darkening evening sky. Dusk arrived. Out of the gloom, diving at blurring speed into the chimney, a solid cloud-sized swarm of swallows, thousands of them, tens of thousands, descend from the sky... a time stopping, two minute manic rush into the chimney. Then, silence. Tomb silence... until dawn and the exodus in reverse.

You have all seen these miracles of nature. What do they tell us, these magical moments?

The grand scheme of the universe offers wonders beyond the orderly routines of our daily lives. When we stumble across them, and ponder them, these singular moments, we are graced with a flash of insight into the miracle of life itself. We can see our own life as the miracle it is. We become humbled by the experience... and exalted at the same time, illuminated by the vision of the world, interconnected, ant, dolphin, barn swallow... YOU.

The next time you are bored with a task, recall the miracles you have witnessed. Ponder the yogic saying, "We all can see the drop as part of the ocean; we must strive to see the ocean in the drop." Consider the meaning of this Buddhist axiom, "The entire world is found in a Zen garden."

WHAT'S IN A NAME?
EVERYTHING!

Every tradition has its way of naming a baby. Often the new arrival is named after a beloved family member, living or deceased, or perhaps the name represents an attribute that the parents respect or want to endow in their heir, such as Charity, Felicity or Richmond (literally, "Richness"). Check the etymology and you'll find that Albert is 'noble,' Berthold is 'bright' and Alexander is 'strong.' The intention is to give the baby a name that will inspire him or her to fulfill their potential... or perhaps serve as a daily reminder of the place where the flame of love caught fire, as in River Phoenix, Orlando Bloom or Paris Hilton.

We think of tagging our kids with inspirational given names in the hope that the name will fulfill the destiny we envision for them. But what if you, as an adult, decide to take on a new name for yourself.

A new name might have a profound effect; literally influencing us to redefine our own destiny by guiding us to new pathways to follow on our life's journey.

Perhaps you've read the series of books entitled *What Would the Buddha Do?* or heard people struggling with a difficult decision ask, "What would Jesus do?" The question being asked is, "What would my higher self do?" as personified in the name of the petitioner's own particular religious or spiritual guide.

In the Kundalini Yoga tradition, one can request a spiritual name that represents your highest destiny, your guiding force. My spiritual name is Santmukh Kaur, which translated means "the princess who has the projection of a saint." Initially, because I didn't intend to use this exotic name in my everyday life, I didn't think much of its significance. Shortly afterward, however, I became a bit frazzled and overwhelmed at the prospect of a potentially difficult family interaction. I recall actually crying and feeling totally helpless until somehow I reminded myself to ask, "What would Santmukh do?" Almost immediately I felt calmed and confident. The everyday part of me known as Arlene was overwhelmed temporarily, but the inner self – the princess who radiates saintliness – knew exactly what to do and behaved accordingly. Elevated to my higher Self, the event turned out to be totally delightful.

Choose a character trait that you feel you would like to have and research the etymology to find a name that fits it (or simply make up a name). Each time an important decision is demanded of you, silently refer to yourself by that name and note its influence on the choice you make. Your spiritual name is your own Green Hornet ring or personal X-man power, adding a new level of "extra" ability to call upon when you lack confidence or feel anxious or fearful when facing uncertainty. In practical ways it can guide you when responding to problems on the job, give you confidence when you're standing over a putt, calm you as you give your presentation to the board of directors. More importantly, when facing the moral dilemmas and ethical decisions that define you as a person, you can ask, "what would my higher self do?" Instead of feeling like a frightened Freddy or nervous Nancy, you can call upon the hidden power that resides within you to give you the answer... and to become the person you believe yourself to be.

THE GOLD TO BE FOUND IN SILENCE

All around us, every day, we hear the babble, blare and bluster, the cacophony, chatter and clamor, the racket, rattle and roar of noise. It's not good for us. Elevated noise levels can create stress and stimulate aggressive behavior. Even low-level noise has been associated with increased aggression, as well as poor sleep, high blood pressure, and heart disease. Kids who live in noisy homes often have a heart rate higher by 2 beats than children from quieter families! What might be even more damaging when constantly surrounded by noise is the difficulty in hearing what is going on inside of us – tuning in to our inner voice.

Silence leads to stillness (there is a subtle difference in meaning) and it is that stillness that enables you to hear all that is important. What a paradox. In the nothing there is everything! Just as the sum total of our awareness of the external world represents but a small fraction of what we call Knowledge, an entire universe lies deep within us, waiting to be discovered and experienced.

Typically, our inner life is different from our outer life. It is misleading to judge someone's inner life by what you see on the outside. One can look cool and collected, have all the trappings of material wealth, and yet feel anxious and sad. The quest is to have one's inner and outer lives in alignment – only then is it possible to live in true harmony.

Are you ready to know yourself better? To interpret the truth behind your feelings? To discover what it is you really want to do in the years that lie ahead? The answers can be found when you turn off the noise and spend time without distraction, without talking to anyone or listening to any outside intrusions. Creativity is born in Silence. Sitting in repose, slowing your rate of breathing, allows you to listen to the music of your heart. We continuously use energy while thinking, speaking and careening through the day bouncing from one chore to the other. Within this chaos, it is imperative to set aside time for silence. (Gandhi used to spend one day of each week in silence because he believed that abstaining from speaking brought him inner peace.) When you find yourself unconsciously immersed in distraction – the car radio turns on with the ignition; you habitually eat dinner while watching television - set aside a portion of your hectic time clock and gift yourself a measure of silence. Driving to work in silence can create a space where you can get in touch with your thoughts and be with yourself; mindful eating helps you enjoy your food more and prevent overeating because you are tuned in to your body's satiety signals, allowing your body to metabolize food more efficiently. Spend just a few minutes each day in silence, listening to the everyday noises, a clock ticking, birds chirping, and then listen to your own breath. See what happens!

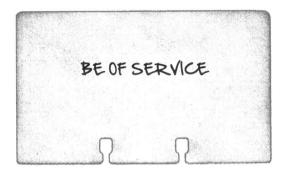

BE OF SERVICE

On a past Christmas Eve, my husband and I were among the men and women at First Saint Paul's Church serving dinner to the homeless. The feast, which is free and open to all, is an annual event. Each year volunteers prepare a traditional turkey dinner with all the fixings for close to two hundred itinerant people living on the streets of Chicago. Above the door to the dining room a volunteer had written "Little will be gained in a lifetime until a person opens his heart wholly and loves all human beings as his own self."

As the line formed, my husband and I wondered if we could open our hearts completely. He was the 'yam man' in the buffet line and I was the lady spooning out the dressing. The raggedy men and women were dirty-faced and in need of shampoos and manicures, but more often than not he and I were able to see past the layer of grime. Toothless grins greeted our smiles; a dignified thank you was the typical response to our respectful "May I serve you Sir, or Madam?" Occasionally a surly, ill-tempered clinical outpatient off his meds threatened mayhem for a perceived slur or slight, but for the most part the served and the servers were joined in grace. When the event was over we felt wonderful, flooded in love for our fellow man. We had given two hours of our time to selfless service and received a sense of bliss that money could not buy.

Why does being of service feel so good?

Because when it's not "all about me" we are bypassing the ego, unmindful of the applause we typically solicit to bolster our self-importance. Instead, our sense of self-worth is heightened by an irrefutable axiom, "No one is useless in this world who lightens the burdens of another." (Charles Dickens)

That's the irony: when we give others a helping hand up, we lift ourselves! There's a real sense of joy when we act out of a generosity of spirit over and above our pursuit of personal happiness. We feel empowered. And the feeling doesn't stop there – the spirits of the people you help are bolstered, and passed on… and passed on. I call it, Living in the energy of Universal Love.

Try this approach today. When you're confronted with a choice of action, instead of thinking, "What's in it for me?" ask yourself, "Is this an opportunity to help others?" Whether you make yourself available to a friend or co-worker, or you make time to do volunteer work, commit to being of service. Don't just tsk tsk in sympathy – absorb yourself in the spirit of service as a way of life.

A FIVE MINUTE, DAILY 'SABBATH'

The Exodus portion of the Old Testament tells us that six days we shall work but the seventh day shall be hallowed. The commandment is an admonition to reflect on ancient wisdom, celebrate creation and remember our unity with God. The intention is "to stop the world" and meditate and contemplate the universal energies that bring us into harmony with one another and the 'sacred mystery' of the universe. My view is, to do so it's not unequivocally necessary to attend a church or temple and to set aside an entire day to celebrate the abundant blessings of our life. We can take part of every day and consciously give ourselves over to a grateful celebration of the blessings in our life.

As little as five-minutes would make a difference, a "mini Sabbath," so to speak, to remind us of our life in spirit. If we can discipline ourselves to truly stop, really commit ourselves to a period of reflection, it needn't take long to restore a sacred rhythm to the day, to balance time in the outer world with time in the inner. It is more important to be consistent in putting time aside for spiritual contemplation than to log the hours as if to prove your 'goodness.'

As part of my breakfast routine, for example, I follow this practice. Before drinking my tea I raise my cup in tribute to all the participants who contributed to the savory brew – the clerks who stocked the grocery shelves, the drivers who trucked it to the stores, the workers who packaged it, the farmers who grew the tea to the elders who taught them how to prepare it. Then I focus on my drink, first noticing the smell, then sipping slowly and relishing the flavor. It's a wonderful daily exercise in mindfulness. (For their formal tea ceremonies, the Japanese often conduct rituals that last up to four hours!)

If in the midst of your hectic day you can commit five minutes to settle yourself in peace and stillness, it will make an enormous difference in how you relate to others and how you conduct yourself throughout the day. When you are at peace, the energy of your physical body takes the shape of what is known as the Divine Will, and you will become more fully aware of who you are and whom you are meant to be.

THE MERGING OF
BODY, MIND AND
SPIRIT

The beauty and elegance of the chakra system is that it is not strictly physical, nor is it completely metaphysical. Instead, it is an absolutely unique confluence of both material and non-material energy. As such, it exists equally in the realms of body, mind, and spirit.

Meditation as Medicine, Dharma Singh Khalsa, M.D.
and Cameron Stauth

The In-Sourcing Handbook provides daily reminders that happiness is not reliant on rewards of the material world. It guides you inward, offering glimpses of life absent ego, aggression and fear. Now the question is, are you ready to go deeper?

A Handbook is not a 'textbook.' It's a convenient, concise ready reference, a guide to making things work when they break down. It tells you where to get the parts and how to install them. And it stops there, its purpose fulfilled when the problem is fixed and the motorcycle or vacuum cleaner is up and running.

The mechanic looks at a schematic, adjusts the airfoils on a jet's wings and the plane returns to the air. To truly know why and how the plane flies, however, there is more to be learned, information that is not found in the 'fix it' handbook, but in science and theory... it is nature's abhorrence of a vacuum that lifts the plane into the sky.

Similarly, there is a complex law of nature that must be mastered prior to attaining what the yogis know as 'enlightenment' or the ultimate happiness. As they have taught us throughout the ages, a subtle body made up of energy centers, called chakras, resides within us in harmony with our physical form. Essentially it is the unseen force that animates us – literally makes us alive. All of you who have ever been in the room with a dying family member or friend will have no doubt about its existence. For me it became obvious when I saw my 95-year-old mother just after she had died. Instead of the sleeping woman there was a waxen image. The vital life force was gone, as if someone just turned off the light switch and the room went dark.

The human chakra system was described by yogic sages thousands of years ago (chakra is a Sanskrit word meaning 'wheel') and has proven to be a surprisingly accurate roadmap to our physical, psychological and spiritual health - and ultimately, our highest degree of 'innate knowledge,' a state of pure bliss often referred to as 'cosmic consciousness.' Have I ever achieved it? I've come close. Every once in a while, when lost in deep meditation or immersed in a gong bath after strenuous yoga exercise, I get a delicious taste of what it's like to feel awash in peaceful contentment, independent of both criticism and praise from others. Afterward the blissful feeling spills over into my everyday life, shining light on my work, family and relationships with others.

The phenomenon is experiential. Like riding a bike, one can't 'know' what it is like to achieve balance until one actually *is* balanced on the bike and riding without falling. No amount of reading about the occurrence can 'teach' you to achieve balance. Similarly, the investigation of the subtle body is beyond the purview of the *In-Sourcing Handbook*. Exploration of the chakra system and the life force it creates is a journey to the doorway of divinity, a stage of evolution deeper than most of us shall ever achieve, beyond Body, Mind and Spirit standing alone as 'source.'

Here are a few of the masters I urge you to become acquainted with as you begin your journey: Carolyn Myss, author of *Anatomy of the Spirit,* the epochal introduction to an exploration of the chakras; Deepak Chopra, a prolific writer of dozens of books about a benevolent universe where love, health and happiness are possible; Anodea Judith, whose wonderful book, *Wheels of Life* is a lucid and inspiring description of the chakras.

These enlightening books and dozens of others will introduce you to the chakra system and 'the great truth' they reveal - we all live in harmony connected to an everlasting, celestial universe that lies beyond our finite existence. A brief outline of the fundamentals follows:

The first, or root chakra (color red) is at the base of the spine and connects us to the earth, encompassing our basic needs of survival. Aspects of Inner Happiness – a sense of security and stability.

The second (color orange) is just below the navel and addresses sexuality, procreation and the birth of ideas. Aspects of Inner Happiness – exuberance for life, sensuality, sexuality and creativity.

The third (color yellow) is at the solar plexus and is the energy center of our personal power. Aspects of Inner Happiness – individuality and, independence; vitality.

The fourth or heart chakra (color green) is where compassion and unconditional love are sourced. Aspects of Inner Happiness - relationships and service.

The fifth (color blue) is at the throat and affects authentic communication and self-expression. Aspects of Inner Happiness – creativity.

The sixth, the so-called third eye (indigo or purple) is found between the eyebrows and is our place of intuition; of knowing beyond the known. Aspects of Inner Happiness - dreams, imagination and visualization.

The seventh, the crown chakra (color white or violet) is just above the top of our head and is our spiritual connection

to the universal consciousness. Aspects of Inner Happiness
- self-realization; enlightenment.

Are you intrigued? I know that without factual, proof-positive
evidence rooted in secular science one can remain dubious of the existence of the so-called metaphysical world. But the Inner Happiness we
seek is not defined by data and lab tests. By those criteria the miracle
of a glorious sunset is merely light refracting off dust particles in the
atmosphere! I think it is something more.

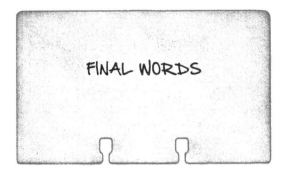

FINAL WORDS

Finding your own inner happiness is your triumph, yours alone. It speaks to your individual strength of character and your personal integrity. These are the attributes that reside within you and provide the foundation for the inner happiness that expands exponentially with each pathway you set out on and complete.

Some days will be harder than others. Frequently you'll be tempted to quit along the way; your friends and family may look at you askance and belittle your endeavor. Here is how I deal with the potential stumbling blocks: I take a deep breath and survey each situation with a SOLID scrutiny:

    S – Stop
    O – Observe
    L – Listen
    I - Integrate
    D - Do

It takes only a few moments to pause and appraise the situation, and to renew my commitment. Learning how to think before acting creates space to become responsible for both the reward and consequences of the choices we make, and to renounce the unhealthy role of "victim of circumstance". All you really need for inner happiness is your breath and your conscious awareness. All the rest is commentary. When we learn to rely on ourselves and to love ourselves, we live lives of joy and fulfillment —we are happy!

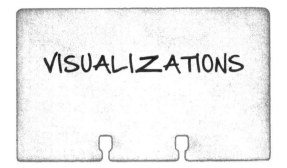

VISUALIZATIONS

In-sourcing is a way to connect to your own wisdom. In the process it's necessary to clear away the negative energy that bedevils us, and create balance – the place where calmness and inner peace provide space for contemplation and wisdom. The following visualizations will balance your energy and replace negative energy with the positive, allowing you to move calmly though the day, your inner wisdom on call as needed.

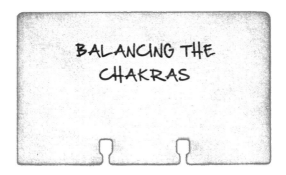

BALANCING THE
CHAKRAS

1.Sit quietly with your spine straight.

2.Consciously breathe four repetitions as follows:
   Inhale for 4 counts – Hold for 1 count
   Exhale for 8 counts – Hold for 4 counts

3.Put a 'Grounding Cord' in place as follows:

Start at the base of the spine and imagine a cord tied
to the base of your spine and extending down to
the center of the earth where it is securely hooked,
grounding you firmly in place. (In my office, to show
the effectiveness of this visualization, I ask my client
to stand up and if they would allow me to gently push
them at their shoulders. They often are wobbly. Then
I ask them to set their grounding cord, I give a little
push, and they are strong and firm).

4. Review the location of each chakra:

> 1st: base of the spine
> 2nd: few inches below the belly button
> 3rd: just below the breast bone, at the solar plexus
> 4th: the heart center
> 5th: base of the throat
> 6th: between the eyebrows
> 7th: approximately four inches above the crown of the head

5. With the grounding cord keeping you firmly rooted, balance each of the seven chakras as follows:

> Imagine the familiar Scales of Justice or Apothecary scale.
> For each chakra, notice if the scale is in or out of balance.
> If it is out of balance, set the intention to restore it to equilibrium and do so by using your breathing to manifest that intention.

When all the chakras are in balance you have easy access to your inner wisdom. Ask the question for which you want an answer. Sit quietly, and wait for the insight that will lead you to the appropriate answer.

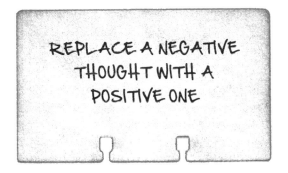

REPLACE A NEGATIVE
THOUGHT WITH A
POSITIVE ONE

1.Find a comfortable place to sit upright and close your eyes.

2.Take several relaxing breaths (inhale 4, hold 1, exhale 8, hold 4) and imagine a ground cord going from the base of your spine to the center of the earth.

3.See your negative belief about yourself as if it was on an old piece of parchment and notice the age you were when you signed and agreed to it.

4.Look in the eyes of the child that you were and notice what she/he is feeling.

5.Notice where in your body you have the sensation of that feeling and rate it from 1-10, ten being the highest.

6.Give the feeling a color and a shape and keep breathing and watching it until it automatically dissipates. (You don't have to "try", just watch and it will get very big and dissipate or very small and disappear).

7.When it is released, pick a color that represents the positive feeling that you now have and imagine it flowing down from the top of your head, throughout your body and expanding even beyond your physical body, creating a colorful aura all around you.

8.Now place that old document at least 10' outside the colorful aura and imagine you are striking a match and setting it aflame. Watch until all that remains is a pile of ash.

9.Place your hand on your heart center, the center of your chest, and imagine a door at the center of your back, behind where your hand it placed.

10.Enter into your sacred heart center from the back door, and walk until you find the most sacred spot. (If there is tension in your heart center, breathe it out).

11.Look around and find a blank piece of paper and a pen waiting for you at this sacred spot…and from this peaceful place write a new statement about yourself. (Write in the first person, present tense and make sure there are no negative words in the statement).

12. Invite your younger self, the child you were, to join you. When both of you agree the new statement is acceptable (that means there is no tension in your body and you see/hear the words), sign the new agreement and store it in your heart center, so that you can always remember it "by heart."

THE AUTHORS' JOURNEYS

There have been many chapters to my life—as I am sure there have been in your lives as well. Getting older has the advantage of looking back, gaining perspective from atop a hill to see where I have been, affirm where I am now and get a sense of where I will be going. This perspective helps me integrate all the disparate parts of my life and allows me to integrate them into a coherent whole with a deepening understanding of how and where happiness resides.

My former tenure as an English teacher enables me to make sense of the structure, symbolism and metaphors behind the personal narratives my clients share with me. My years in the business world as a proprietor of a chain of children's' clothing stores are equivalent to having a hands-on

MBA, learning the principles of marketing, accounting and lots of left-brain skills, which serve me well in my therapy practice. As an executive director for a community organization I learned to recognize how the individual interacts within his social environment, clearly important in doing therapy. I was in my mid-40's when I completed the graduate program that prepared me for the therapy practice I've maintained for the past twenty-plus years.

I learned traditional talk therapy at Jewish Family & Children's Services of Chicago, employing the important social work principles... beginning where the client is... accepting the reality of "what is"...and seeing the client as part of his own unique emotional, physical, cultural and familial systems. Recognizing the stressors originating within these systems taught me to see my clients not as 'sick patients,' but rather as human beings dealing with the stresses intrinsic to their lives.

My foray into less traditional treatments started in 1996 with the beginning of my hypnotherapy training at the renowned Wellness Institute of Issaquah, Washington. During those years I was introduced to breath work, Siddha yoga (meditative yoga), psychodrama, and Kundalini yoga. It is my continuing study of Kundalini Yoga that sustains me presently. Many of the references in this Handbook have origins originated from this discipline. Yogi Bhajan brought the ancient teaching of Kundalini yoga to the west in 1968. He died in 2004 but his impact continues today.

The view from a top of the hill shows me how I have come full circle. My parents wanted me to become a teacher—and I have, but not in the form they envisioned. The oath I took at the completion of my Kundalini yoga teacher training is "I am not a woman, I am not a man, I am not a person, I am not myself...I am a teacher."

This Handbook is my way of teaching you to go beyond self-imposed limitations, journeying inward where the source of true happiness is found.

Sat Nam (My True Self)
Arlene Englander

The path that Arlene is traveling has ample room for a companion. I follow along in her footsteps, accompanying her to the workshops where spouses and significant others are invited to participate. The atmosphere is loving and supportive; the facilitators gentle and caring; my resistance vanishes as I sink into a space of deep relaxation, a trance state where the heart is the hub of all sacred places and the spirit roams. We meditate; we chant; we craft Indian drums from deer skins and build a sweat lodge where a Native American Indian guides us to the earth's four directions. As I learn to "let go," to yield to the sway of shamans and saints, there are times, magical times, when I too, experience the glow. Assisting her in the writing of the *In-Sourcing Handbook, Where and How to Find the Happiness You Deserve*, has been a learning event as no other!

I've been retired for many years but have no interest in the early bird special at the pancake house. After a life-long career in advertising and marketing, I remain active writing about the realities of aging, making it a point to debunk the Hollywood and television stereotypes of "the grumpy old man" and "the ditzy grandma." Available on <u>www.Amazon.com</u> as a printed or Kindle digital book, my collection of short stories entitled "73," probes the true feelings, inevitable problems and unexpected opportunities that lie ahead for America's growing senior population. As the stories vividly express, when old age hits, you can either fall down or hit back. I recently finished a follow-up to 73, entitled *Behind Every Wrinkle There's a Story.*

Sat Nam
Howard Englander

May the long time sun shine upon you
All love surround you
And the pure light within you
Guide your way on.
Sat Nam

The *Longtime Sunshine* is sung at the end of each Kundalini Yoga session as the farewell blessing. It was written by a Scottish, psychedelic folk group called *The Incredible String Band.*

www.wellnesssource.com
www.howardenglander.com